STANDING IN THE MIDDLE OF THE ROAD

STANDING IN THE MIDDLE OF THE ROAD

A Poetry Collection

MARY EMMA TISINGER

Clovercroft Publishing

Standing in the Middle of the Road: A Poetry Collection

Published by Clovercroft Publishing, Franklin, Tennessee
www.clovercroftpublishing.com

Cover and Interior Jonathan Lewis

Printed in the United States of America

ISBN (hardcover): 978-1-956370-78-2
ISBN (paperback): 978-1-956370-83-6

Contents

Down the Road

Up the Road

Welcome to *My Road*

MY DAUGHTER, LISA, and her husband Travis have a house in Wachapreague, Virginia. Wachapreague is a little fishing town, nestled along the Chesapeake, just before the Chesapeake Bay bridge tunnel opens wide its mouth to swallow travelers, carry them through the waters of the Bay, and spit them out on the other side.

When Lisa calls from Wachapreague to my home in Dover, almost always she's standing in the middle of the road, the street that runs in front of their house. She's found that to be the place she can get the best reception on her cell phone, enabling us to talk to each other. It's a safe place since traffic is light, rarely does a vehicle approach, and the view is good. One can see in all directions.

When Lisa calls we laugh about the fact that she's standing in the middle of the road. However, aren't we all—*standing in the middle of the road?*

The road of life extends forward and backward. Forward, to those many and varied experiences that await us (times of happiness, sadness, grief, regret, even despair).

And backward, down the road, to previous events, times, and places, where life before has taken us.

At any given moment it seems we're either standing still, engrossed in what we're doing; or thinking about where we've been; or contemplating the future. Our past is behind us; our future, ahead.

And the road, below.

Wealth I ask not, hope nor love,
Nor a friend to know me;
All I ask, the heaven above
and the road below me.

The Vagabond
Robert Louis Stevenson

When Here

When, here, I stand,

the road below me,

forward, I see,

and back.

The choice is mine . . .

whether to stand still,

or perhaps, move ahead;

up the road

to what lies beyond

or down the road

to a former place,

an earlier time:

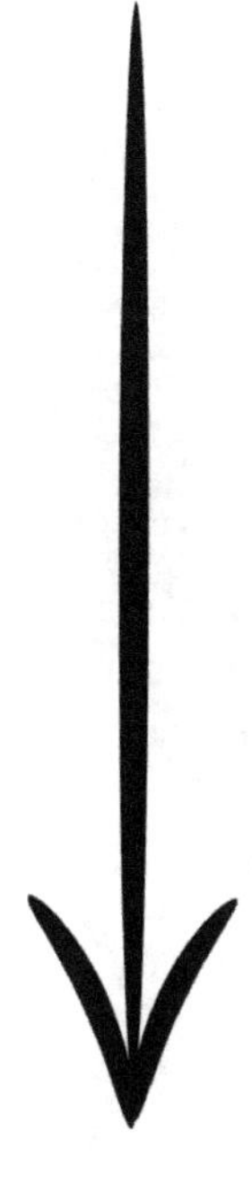

to Yesterday

Down the Road

Where the Road before Has Taken Me

Grandson Grown

The smile was just the same
as that of the three-year-old
who did not want me to leave that day
so long ago, when I was visiting
and it was time to go.

So cute then,
as three-year-olds insist on being,
he ran to a dining room chair,
patted it down
and "Sit," he said.

Still as endearing today
as he was then;
though no longer two feet tall,
but six;
and no longer three,
but twenty-four;

my hand he held so I wouldn't fall
as we left the doctor's office
this morning,
and that little black bubble
kept bouncing around in my eye.

Roots

Her words, "Oh, *I AM* someone else," settled
between my ears and there they stayed, when I,

(mistaking her for someone I thought I knew),
smiled and said hello. Up close, her sun-tinged

hair and pixie face signaled a stranger, she;
but cause to wonder she gave to me. Not

about her, but about me. Am I, too . . .
someone else, and not the person I presume to be?

This sand, these shores, may I claim as my own?
Now that I've given all these years to clouds

wind-blown in skies that smell of the sea,
and strolled the sands along the Atlantic.

In years gone past when first he asked, these words
were mine: *Where in the world is Delaware?*

And now I call the "first state" home. But my
southern roots I can't disown: the magnolia

sweet, nor the Carolina "tar" that so
closely clings to both my feet; and not to

mention the syrupy drawl that some call
twang—all are mine. Even so, it seems my

earthy roots into the ocean have grown;
and between my toes, drifting sand from a

thousand shores has found a home; while arrogant
seagulls ever-circle 'round my head; and

the salty spray from blue-green waves
slides gently down my cheek . . .

the tar on my heels remains.

Lost

where is my mother
I search for my mother

I look in every room
she is not there

I go next door
I climb the long steps upward

I do not see her
no one answers the door

I sit on the steps
I cry for my mother

later she comes, she is angry
angry that I looked for her

that I did not stay in my room
as I was supposed to do

I don't like to lose my mother

At Times, They Fight

she yells at him
he yells at her

I sit next to her
my baby sister on her lap

my brother on the chair
next to the wall

anger stifles the air
choking my throat

my head aches
my tummy hurts

I don't understand
why does my father

yell at my mother
tears roll down my cheeks

The Chill

in the November air
my thin sweater
barely keeps me warm

go outside and play
momma said
'til dinner is ready

but the air is chill
it is not so warm
and there's nothing to do

from the building
next to the house
someone calls

hey kids, come over here
the jail window is small
bars hide his face

we don't go near
we wait
for our mother's call

Don't Ask

sometimes when she comes
to our house

she gives us gum
my brother my sister and I

we love the sweet taste
and it lasts for hours

'til momma says, spit it out
when it's time for bed

today when she came
there was no gum

aunt emma, I said
do you have any gum

later, the spanking hurt
I don't understand

why my father said
we don't ask for gum

A Father's Love

Did he?
I think he did . . .
but he never said.

They always vowed I was his favorite,
Daddy's pet!
Was it the shared ancestral scent
of Ireland in our genes?
Blonde hair like his? And eyes of blue?
"Sibling rivalry," Momma said.
But how could she tell
if no words were said?

Did he?
I think he did . . .
Isn't that what fathers do?

Why, then,
would he chase Santa down the street
for a bag of treats for a five-year-old,
too shy to sit on Santa's knee?
Why, then,
would he stand proud and tall
when his daughter led the class, ranking
first of all, graduation day;
then make it a point to hang around
the night before she went away,
college-bound?

But then . . .
Where was he on her wedding day?
Or the birth of his grandchild . . . one, two, and three?

It was after his stroke, on his hospital bed,
eyes interlocked, but no words were said;
for his speech was gone, and soon was he.

Did he?
I think he did, but . . .
he never said.

The Seventh of December

It was a Sunday afternoon, sunny,
cold and wintry, typical December;
a "getting-close-to-Christmas" kind of day.

We crowded into the car, the seven of us,
for a trip to the big city, miles away.
Christmas shopping for Momma, big sister Alene,

and "whatever" for Daddy and Uncle George.
And—hopes and dreams of popcorn and lollipops
for my brother, my sister, and me.

No sooner had we arrived and started down the street,
admiring Christmas all around,
when Daddy and Uncle George came running,

ushered us quickly back to the car;
we were going home. The grown-ups spoke
in whispers, their tension hard to hide;

anxiety filled the car, squeezing out all the air.
My mother's arms tightened around me
as the words over the radio came:

The bombs keep falling . . . and falling!
Pearl Harbor is under attack!
America, we are at war!

We Watched and We Waited

'Twas a game we used to play,
huddled together on the front porch swing,
on those days when we expected
a trip into town,
or at least to the general store;

where a kindly old gentleman behind the counter
would dig into the fishbowl
next to the register, and bring out lollipops
or some other sweet treat for us to enjoy.
If Momma would allow.

So we watched and we waited
and we sang our little rhyme,
Here comes Daddy!
Here comes Daddy!
'Twas a magical chant that in our childish minds

we believed would bring Daddy home;
as we watched and we waited, ever hoping
next to see . . . our old gold Chevy,
reeking body odor of sweat and the weather,
rounding the bend.

It was no big thing, just a trip to the market
for bread and milk, staples;
but for us . . . it was *Disney World.*
So we watched and we waited
and we sang our little rhyme

(which worked almost never);
while inside the house
Momma fretted and fumed,
'til finally we could shout,
"Momma, he's here!"

Water Knows No Color

Back then, we trudged up the hill; two small children,
a boy and his sister, carrying a bucket
with instructions to ask, *Please, may we draw*
from your well? Although we were different
in race and skin color, we all drank from the same
old, gray metal bucket, water of no color,
we drew from their well. Color didn't matter,
they had a well, and they knew we had none.

Today, violence, unrest, fill the streets of the city.
There's rioting and looting and flames that
leap upward—from a rage burning deep within.
And I weep . . . I weep for my sister, my brother,
who cry "peace and justice," and—for those two
small children back then. Those two who asked, *Please,*
may we draw from your well? Mindful of how
we all drink from the same old, gray metal bucket,
water of no color—no matter the color our skin.

Affirmation

I have loved you every day of my life.
your words

words I will never forget
locked within my heart

to lift out
time and time again

to treasure
and then restore

until those times
I need once more

a reminder
reassurance

affirmation
of your love

Where Roses Bloomed

Once roses bloomed
around my window sill,
fragrance, sweet;
green, the grass;
sunshine, bright.

The clouds
that sometimes dimmed the blue above
soon were gone;
life was complete,
while still the roses bloomed.

But then,
one cool and crispy morn
I found the roses crumpled on the ground,
and I knew,
nevermore

would I enjoy the beauty,
nor the velvet softness of the touch.
Gone,
the sweet, sweet essence;

scattered,
the fragile petals;
where once
the roses bloomed.

By The Hearth[1]

His chair, with stripes of burgundy, green
and tan, (not so straight now, after years
of being leaned against,
or sat upon),
still hugs the space nearby.
The smothering odor of wood smoke
lingers,
while the glass enclosure, shut when he left
and never reopened,
reflects the light of the reading lamp
on the table by the side.
My eyes begin to sting
and blur,
as yet, I see him
sitting there.

Come Christmas, I'll put pine cones and holly
on the mantle.

The Shadow Waltz

I watch the shadows play
upon my bedroom door;
up and down,
back and forth,
intense,
diminishing;

from light to dark,
from bright to dim;
and then, with steps retraced,
they dance their merry waltz again.

Like shadows on my bedroom door,
you dance around the edges of my life;
sometimes bright,
sometimes dim,
sometimes close,
approaching;

and then
you back away,
and I'm alone—
again.

Peonies She Loved

(in memory of Joan)

It was summer when first he brought her home
to meet the family; nature's summer, also hers.
Happy her smile as she gave to me the flowers . . .
a potpourri of pink, white, rose and green,
plucked from the peony bush outside her home.

Peonies she loved,
peonies she gave to me.

That first Christmas, her laugh, as she opened her gift,
the dress I had *so hoped* she would like.
Shades of purple with a touch of white.
The dress, she loved;
the joy of giving, mine.

Family dinners, picnics,
birthday celebrations,
the trip to Longwood with Aline in a wheelchair . . .
mysteries,
history,
her pets,
Delmar,
her East Street home . . .

all these she loved.
Peonies she gave to me.

Joan, I will remember . . .
I wish we could have had more time.

Or Almost

The house looked the same. Or almost.
I knew there was no life behind those walls.

Off the roof, a torn welcoming flag
waved forlornly over the front porch.

Several notices: *No Trespassing,* perhaps,
covered the window of the gray door;

there was no lock and key. In the yard,
weeds and overgrowth had been cleared away,

giving the place a cleaner look; and
in the sketchy frozen grass, reminiscent

of all the cats that had been so frequent there,
a life-size mold of a kitten lay.

There was no activity, no stirring around,
no signs of life. The house sat empty, waiting . . .

The two who walked those floors,
climbed those stairs, and at times

rushed out the front door, off the porch
and down the steps in the morning sun,

late for work, or almost . . .
were no longer there.

We Dance to the Music

(in memory of Debbie)

"I really like these," she says,
pointing to the narrow, dark blue,
polka-dotted band around her head.

Nonchalant, she leans against the counter,
burgundy shirt, dark slacks loose
upon her slightly-reduced-by-chemo frame.

But, one only has to glance
at her bare head
to see the battle raging within.

Blond hair gone, but not that sweet,
lovely smile that makes one feel
all cozy and warm, like the sun,

shining on the kitchen floor
in the morning;
while the heavy aroma of bacon,

popping and sizzling on the burner,
wraps itself around.
And then,

kicking out one foot as dancers do,
she reveals her dark blue polka-dotted socks.
"See?" She smiles.

"How together I am?"

Barrett Warner Comes to Dover[2]

I drove to *Roma's,*
wondering . . .
would I be glad in the doing?
I was not disappointed.
He looked like someone
who *could* plant horses
and watch them grow,
which he said he does, but
he spoke as poets speak.
Scattered Van Gogh's and Picasso's
around the room with his words,
and seemed like an old friend
in less than an hour. Not in the least
someone you would turn off
and draw daisies and tulips
on your napkin.
And he did all this
with a hand once kicked off
by a horse.

Hummingbirds

For a few brief moments the hummingbird,
so small he could fit into one's hand,
hovers 'round the flower,
and then he's gone.

"Happens at all times during the day," she says.
"He's always humming a hymn he used to sing.

And it doesn't scare me," she says,
"because I know it's him."

"But why," she says, why can't others
hear his humming too?"

Problem is, a few weeks ago, she watched
as they lowered his cold, gray casket into the ground.

I wonder, could this be her way of holding on to him,
'cause she just can't bear facing life alone?

And yet, *she surely must know,*
like the hummingbird, one day he will move on;

it's the whirring of his wings we hear,
and not his song.

Shadows

I live among the shadows.
They're always around,

even on dismal days when the sun
hides behind the clouds,

or water drips from the heavens
at a slow, steady pace all day long.

At times, the shadows run ahead,
beckoning me to follow.

Often, they move slowly,
quietly, by my side,

on the way to wherever.
Or trail along behind.

Constant companions now, I pray
they never slide down into the grave.

Shadows are part of living, they say,
for those who truly love.

Dying to Write

I laughed when he said,
"You don't have to die

to write about death."
'Twas funny, just to think

of a dead man writing.
But then I remembered

the day that it happened,
and I knew he was wrong.

It was cold, like December;
there was ice on the pavement

and snow in the air.
I watched as you lingered,

and your life ebbed away . . .
like the tide, sliding slowly

out to the sea.
No, it wasn't for me,

Death came calling in the winter,
but when he left

he took with him . . . my heart,
and a huge part of me.

Midnight, Christmas Eve

The tree still stands in its usual place;
lights shine bright in the balsam green,
casting a glow on the Christmas balls
scattered up and down the tree.
The tree skirt swirls around the base
and the presents, all wrapped,
are in place,
ready for Christmas morn.
But it's not the same.

For I sit alone in the darkened room,
remembering Christmas past,
when you sat with me.
Body-tired were we,
but our hearts were filled
with Christmas peace,
and the joy of giving
to those we love.

I close my eyes
and I see your face,
and for one brief moment
feel the warm embrace of your arm
around my shoulders
once again;
and wish you were here,
to watch with me
at midnight,
on Christmas Eve.

Guilty

The young man stood at the counter,
an energy drink and a snack
waited for payment,
but his credit card would not work.

Next in line, I felt a nudging in my heart,
Pay for his drink and his snack,
said that still, small voice.
But . . . I hesitated.

After a moment or two the clerk
came around and tried to help;
still the card would not work.
The young man walked away,
head down, shoulders slumped,
out into the excessive heat
of the August day.

Pushing aside the energy drink and the snack
the young man *could have had,*
the clerk looked deep into my eyes
and painted an invisible "G" on my forehead
for the guilt that was in my heart.
"Next?" she said.

But it was your voice I heard, Lord,
your words when you said:
Inasmuch as you have not done it
unto the least of these, my brethren,
you have not done it
unto me.

Road Signs

Through the years, many times
this road I've traveled,
without mishap, until today.

Markers were gone,
huge machines blocked the way.
I was lost, wandering,

and wondering,
Where do I go? Which way
is the right way?

I followed all the rules,
obeyed all the signs,
yet, the road

I could not find.
Someone, somewhere,
moved the markers.

The Scent of Lilacs

Shadowed now, the night, so dark,
will slowly fade away,
and morning's golden light gentle in,
to dawn anew another day;
and in the wind, the scent
of lilacs.

Fragrant, heady,
leaves of green,
announcing yet, another spring;
lilacs, you gave to me.

Outback, still, the lilacs bloom,
profuse in lavender and sweet perfume.
And though you've gone,
I close my eyes, I see you near;
and once again you offer me
a sweet bouquet of love.

Pandemic Summer

Locked into my off-white walls and rose-colored carpet,
the hours pass. *Will it ever end?*
Outside, on the deck, stretched out on the railing,
a baby gray squirrel warms his small body
in the bright morning sun;

his big bushy tail backed up against siding
the color of pale lemons. Walls
that set him free . . . and bind me in.
Nature's normalcy
in an abnormal world.

Newspapers headline Covid-19:
Seven more deaths, twenty new cases.
Depression hovers outside my door,
eager to pounce on those tired of isolation,
the fear, the solitude, the sameness.

I dream of other summers,
the long, long drive to the shore;
the warm, wet sand beneath my feet;
the soft, gentle brush of ocean spray,
cool against my cheek;

hot dogs, sauerkraut, and the sweet,
sweet taste of Dolle's salt-water taffy
on my tongue . . . as I mingle, hot and sweaty,
with the boardwalk crowd.

Perhaps, in my mask,
I'll take a walk around the block after dinner.

Sunday in the Nursing Home

"I'm here to see an old friend. Could you tell me,
please, where to find her?"
Near the desk an elderly man, eyes closed,
head drooping over his chest,
nods in his wheelchair.

A few steps away, in a motorized chair,
a lady looks up,
white hair neatly combed,
her sweater the color of a cloudless sky
on a sunny day.
The smile-that-almost-was
slowly fades when I turn to say hello.
Quickly she looks away,
fixing her gaze on the long leaf pines outside,
across the way.

I walk down a long hallway,
then another, not quite as long,
wishing all the while that pungent odor
of urine pushing rudely into my face
would go away.

And then I see her, in the social room,
wheelchair backed up against the wall;
a large-screen television blares nearby.
The ninety-one-year-old brown eyes
never leave my face as I move,
dodging inert bodies in their metal cages,
and pause before her.

I see the beginning of a smile.
"Hello," she says.
"Do I know you?"

Bittersweet

White lace and tulle billowed around them.
Her head against his shoulder;
his chin
lightly touching the top of her head,

while his arms wrapped tightly around her—
as though never to let go.
For the moment, once again,
she was his little girl,

bouncing along beside him,
brown hair shining in the sun.
A father, letting go.
A daughter, accepting the change

from a life that was,
to a life that was to be.
Emotion, heady, strong,
filled the room,

choking my throat,
stinging my eyes,
treading my heart,

as the father of the bride
danced with his daughter.
Bittersweet, the tears.

Never to Waste

"You don't waste a minute, do you?" he said.
I smiled. *What a nice thing to say!*
I loved the thought; much nicer than, "Come on!
Hurry up! We're going to be late!"

Wrapping the words into a tight little bundle,
I tied them up tightly, tucked them away in my head,
and slid into the passenger's seat
of the silver Honda Accord.

With a sigh of relief,
he backed the car out of the garage,
while I backed up to those beautiful words
I had just heard,
You don't waste a minute, do you?

Waste a minute?
Minutes are precious . . . innumerable,
like grains of sand along the sea shore,
stems of grass on the front lawn,
or rain drops thudding upon the roof . . .

the stuff life is made of.
Never, to waste.

Up the Road

to times, places, experiences, yet to be . . .

As the Crow Flies

From south to north
as the crow flies,

so they say . . .
but then, who of us

can truly say . . .
how the crow flies?

Who can say
whose black wings those are,

fluttering, gliding, swooping,
in the sky above?

Or whose black eyes those are,
scouring so closely

the terrain down below?
Can you? Can I?

Who, then, can say
if that black bird

flying high above
is truly a crow?

Wachapreague Calling

He gets a little antsy when winter says goodbye
and the weather grows warm;
and before long we see
that "wish-I-were-there"
look in his eye.
Wachapreague calling.

Soon he's out in his boat,
prepping for a trip to the water's edge,
dreaming all the while
of sitting in the sun,
hours on end,
fishing rod in hand.

Is it the lure of the sea
down deep in his blood;
or the tide washing over the sand?
Whatever the draw,
like fishermen of old
he has heard the call . . .
and he *has* to go.

Wachapreague calling.

Waiting for Morning

waiting for the sun to rise
and play his little game
of hide and seek

moving in and out
among the leaves
of the maple trees out back

where the sky settles down
upon the earth
and the sun

his daily round begins
as shades of gray
and the night

fade . . . into nothingness

waiting for the shrill
mechanical voice
of the bedside clock

to shove aside the night
and intrude into
my warm cocoon

where anything goes
time stands still
and nothing seems real

until
the dog does his daily dive
upon my bed and I feel

his warm, wet tongue
upon my skin, panting
waiting

waiting . . . to begin

The Seagulls March at Wachapreague

Arrogant, they march right up
as though they are the ones in charge
at Thirty-Four Whaling Street.
Is it the fish they smell?

Unafraid,
they strut up to the place
where I,
catch of the day, filet.

Heads down,
shoulders straight,
as though on mission bent,
quite regal their attire:

high-collared vests of purest white,
elegant dinner coats of black or gray,
with heads and tails,
an even darker black.

Their cry,
a mournful, grating noise,
which almost seems a question
left unsaid.

Perhaps, that's why.

On Deck

The sun, hot upon my head;
not a ripple stirs the blue-green waters
of the bay.
I wait.

Sooner,
perhaps later,
the fish will bite,
hungry for that morsel of food
that dangles before them.

And then,
caught, the struggle begins.
If I'm lucky,
we'll have flounder for dinner tonight.

Sand Pebbles and Pearls[3]

In the sand by the sea children play,
searching for treasures swept in by the tides

moving steadily,
rhythmically,
naturally,
noisily,
onto the shore.

"Listen, and hear," says the conch,
"the roar of the ocean when I'm held to your ear."

"Pick me up gently," speaks the clam of his shell,
"this is my home, it has served me well."

While the starfish reveals its stellar star shape,
the oyster waits quietly his secret to tell,

that the pearl he holds
is rare and as dear as silver and gold.

Hardly noticed, the sand pebble shines in the sun,
smoothed and refined by water and time

as the tides rush in and slowly recede,
leaving their treasures
in the sand by the sea.

Nightfall

Like the discordant haunting whine
of a tight guitar string,
silence

hammers against my ears
as I lie upon my bed
in the charcoal darkness.

Around my head
the world spins, and whirls:
cars, on the nearby highway;

an airplane, low, overhead;
a lonely owl in the pine tree;
the rustle of leaves outside my window;

the creak of the floor boards
settling in;
the continual tick, tick, tick

of the clock by the bedside; and,
pulsing and throbbing within my chest,
a steady, pounding drumbeat . . .

the beat of life.
I take a deep breath,
and hold.

Summer Solstice

On my head
the sun's hot hands are pressing;
like flimsy rubber bands,
my legs have lost their zing.

The heat seeps through my shirt,
and snuggles;
there to remain, between my breasts,
'til summer has an end

and sweaty August slips away.
"Tis a short, short distance now
'til summer sun no longer
wraps itself around,

and we welcome cooler rays
of fall's bright orb;
chameleon rays, sprayed light and tender
on maple's leaves and those of yonder oak;

leaves now green, doomed to yellow,
brown,
and 'round our feet to huddle,
as we await the winter's cold.

Yet, even so, I know . . .
my fickle heart again will yearn
the warm and sweaty haze
of summer's gold.

August Storm[4]

Sounded like a blast,
that rumble . . .
heavy, deep,
just before the rain.
Could have been a car
banging into another
(happens sometimes),
or maybe an explosion
nearby.
But then the rain came down.

Poured from the roof,
so much so
the gutters overflowed,
and the maples and yews out front,
trembled;
while the leaves flew all around,
searching frantically
for a place to settle
on the wet, soggy
ground.

November Chill

Dry leaves hurry across the lawn,
brown in spots
that not so long ago were garbed in green.

Trees stand naked in the wind,
bare limbs shivering in the cold;
while lively squirrels

scamper off the deck and race across the lawn,
to scramble up the long-leaf pine . . .
to safety, and to home.

A signal
of change to come
as summer fades away,

spawning memories
across the span of time:
apple cider, woodsmoke, outdoor-play,

my mother's call to supper,
chores,
and homework;

and, once again,
I feel the chill of winter
settling in.

To the Rock

you are old
you've been warmed by the sun
cooled by the snow

housed other forms
withstood many storms
yet you remain

what have you seen
what have you heard
come, share with me

all that you know
then I shall be strong
inextinguishable

able to share
parts of myself, yet
remain whole

Appointments, En Masse

The room fills up quickly. Was there a bus?
Or were we all assigned the same appointment time?

Most fit into the box marked "elderly."
Why am I not surprised?

Canes, walkers, and care-givers line up
alongside colonial Queen Annes and highbacks

in their familiar, comforting Williamsburg grays
and blues, as we sit and wait;

wait to see the doctor . . . seeking hope,
seeking healing, seeking wholeness.

Some sit quietly. Some chat with their partner,
friend or relative; and some sit alone. Like me.

Some text, or perhaps it's a game they play
on their iPad or phone. Some read, some fidget;

are they, perhaps, just a little nervous?
Like me?

It's a little like being in church on Sunday morning,
with its rich stained glass of reds, greens, and blues.

There too we wait . . . wait to see the Great Physician,
through prayer, the melodic chords of *Amazing Grace,*

or words of the pastor . . .
seeking hope, seeking wholeness, a better way.

There too are those who sit quietly; those who chat with
relatives or friends; those who text on their iPad or phone;

those who fidget; and those wondering about
that beef stew, simmering with onions, basil, and oregano,

in the crockpot at home.
Lunch waiting.

I close my eyes and I see . . . not angels, nor men and women
in white coats with stethoscopes, but . . .

the Lady in the New York Harbor,
her torch held high.

She's calling the tired, the poor, the yearning masses,
seeking hope, seeking healing, seeking wholeness.

The nurse calls my name and I rise.
I move slowly, quietly, among the masses.

Balloons

In mid-air they hang, suspended,
the red, the white, the blue.
I sit below, in the waiting room . . .

I see planes and ships,
guns and bombs, the flag—star-spangled,
stripes of red, white, and blue.

I see pilgrims, and Indians,
their struggle to survive;
plantations and battlefields,

young men killing and being killed;
greater guns, bigger bombs,
soldiers and sailors . . .

men and women who died
that I might live;
that I might "sit below"

and be reminded
of who we are and
from whence we came.

But then, he comes
with his ladder, and soon
the red, the white, the blue

lie on the floor, replaced by fresher,
brighter hues of white
and green and gold.

Pretty to behold. But . . .
below, I am saddened.
Saddened not to see floating free above,

the red, the white, the blue;
saddened to be reminded
of how quickly change can come,

of how quickly freedom,
and pride of country can be lost.
The lady next to me looks up

from her crossword puzzle book.
"They're really slow today," she says.
"Have you been waiting long?"

Morning, I Smell[5]

magnolias, mimosas
bluebells
and peaches

running barefoot
through the grass
damp with morning dew

feet wet, arms swinging
chasing butterflies
flying low

fluttering, slow and easy
hungry for honeysuckle
growing wild and free

fields of clover
purple
honey bees buzzing

'round the kitchen
breakfast lingers
hominy grits, red-eye gravy

hot coffee, steaming
later, fried chicken
wish-bone pulling

dreaming . . .
Carolina sun, warm
upon my head

Meeting of the Board

They gather 'round the table,
eager to greet
and to be greeted,

to feel an important, valuable part of the club,
of the community,
and of old, historic buildings

with peeling paint and scuffed wooden floors.
They listen to reports,
some lengthy, some short,

some seemingly inconsequential;
pondering all the while
the evening meal,

tomorrow's schedule,
that never-ending list of things undone;
and hope that wintry mix

of sleet and snow
and freezing rain
holds off.

Illusion

Moving slowly and carefully down the long drive
to the uncluttered blacktop
of the street out front,
the Accord leaves tracks in the virgin snow.
A guide for the days ahead, when the air is frigid
and no one comes to shovel,
or lift away the covering
from what lies beneath—crackling and groaning
from the weight of the silver metal—
to reveal,
not the smooth hard ebony of the roadway,
but an uneven icy topping
from the snow of yesterday.
Softness above,
harshness below.

‘Neath Summer Sun

Nights are warm;
warmer, the day,
lingering in the sun;

the blazing sun of summer bright,
when hearts beat strong,
and sweet the song

of honeysuckle,
purple lilac bloom,
robins’ nests, and meadow larks.

Happy, the days,
the carefree days
of summer light;

when children play
barefoot and free
in grasses green

‘neath leafy trees,
while watchful squirrels
lift bushy tails on high.

Thankful, the heart,
the grateful heart
for light, summer’s warmth,
and life.

Heralds

The cicadas sang for me
this morning
as I walked along the path.

Is it true
what people say?

"Heralds, they are,
of the coming cold . . .
fall and winter are on the way."

If so, 'tis sad
to have to say goodbye
to the roses that
'round my window grow;

and to know:
no longer shall I watch
the dainty daisies shyly nod
as I walk by.

Irish Jig

It's the middle of March, St. Patrick's Day;
there's a touch of spring in the air.
The lilacs are budding, beginning to sprout,
the birds are singing and swooping about.
But, shiver me timbers,
it's cold outside!

Seems the old North wind is here to stay;
he huffs and puffs and won't go away.
He tousles my hair, and sets the leaves a-swirl,
then settles them down near the little gray squirrel
who sniffs the air, then scampers away
to his favorite spot in the sun.

Casualty

Like glass, it shines in the morning sun,
wet with the rain of yesterday
and the night before.

From a distance, who could know
it is only a leaf,
separated by the storm,

from the wild rose vine
climbing up,
and around, the railing?

The Pruning

When those rogue green shoots
that extend above
are clipped,
to prune the little tree or shrub,

for a while his limbs lay bare;
he has no covering from the cold
that sweeps the world with frost and snow.

But if strong he stands and does not budge,
just slightly bends to winter's winds,
he stronger grows.

It's in his roots—innate—he knows
spring will come again, and again,
with warmth and sun
and growth.

Snow Bound

The house seems warmer now,
insulated by the snow
piled high on every side,
and on the roof.

The world is white,
pristine white;
no longer green
except for spots

in which sturdy pines
bravely venture to be seen.
I wonder,
do they feel helpless too,

in nature's triumphal move?
Helpless, yes, (would be my guess),
yet powerful,
in the solitude.

Opposites

He smiled, dimple showing,
and watched the rock drop.
Heavy,
it sank fast.

Another pebble,
cotton-light,
sliced through the froth
and disappeared slowly.

April Promise

I gazed through the mesh of the window screen
on the verdant green of April's spring,

the warmth of the sun upon my face.
When suddenly, thunder roared across the sky,

the blue disappeared, the green turned gray,
and raindrops cluttered the wiry mesh,

filling empty spaces, clinging, wet.
Dismayed, I strained my eyes to see

and not lose sight of the pleasant scene;
but raindrops clung to the wiry screen,

distorting my view, glooming my mind,
and my world changed from warm to cool,

from light to dark, in the turbulent storm.
Then, quietly, through the rumbling rain

I heard the faint, small chirp of a baby bird,
spring's forever promise: new life, new hope.

A reminder—God's in his Heaven. He sends
the rain—and beyond the rain, the sun.

Evening Stars

diamonds twinkle
atop black velvet
thrown carelessly across
the deep blue silk
of the evening sky

loveliness above

We Hear A Different Drummer

Let no one say we're slow,
you and I.
Our dance in life
is to a different beat;
and though we seem to plod
we'll reach our goal;
sometimes ahead of those
who scorn our speed,
and thereby
miss the treasures
'round their feet.

Noel[6]

Softly it comes,
enveloping everyone
and everything
with its presence,

like snowfall
quiet and fragile,
beautiful and tender.

Wrapping,
for a brief time,
around the hearts
of those who have waited,
slender ribbons of joy
and peace and love.

And once again
the world remembers a child,
the Christ Child,
born in a manger in Bethlehem

while angels sang
and shepherds in the field
trembled
in awe and wonder.

Christmas.

The End of the Road

A butterfly,
with a bruised wing, am I,
having traveled so long
and thus far.

Fluttering slowly,
may I continue to fly
flower to flower,
the road—life's road—we each must follow.

Whether the road less traveled by,
or a walk with the crowd
on a path well known;
we each must decide
the direction we will go.

I pray to choose wisely,
and at the end of the road,
God willing,
a scent of the flowers
I've touched along the way
will follow.

Notes

Published previously:

1. By the Hearth, *Bay to Ocean 2018,* Eastern Shore Writers Association, Inc., c. 2018, p. 158.
2. Barrett Warner Comes to Dover, *Bay to Ocean 2018,* Eastern Shore Writers Association, Inc., c. 2018, p. 159.
3. Sand Pebbles and Pearls, *Through the Leaves that Fall,* Fruitbearer Publishing, LLC, copyright 2016, p. 36.
4. August Storm, *Bay to Ocean 2018,* Eastern Shore Writers Association, Inc., c. 2018, p. 160.
5. Morning, I Smell, *Bay to Ocean Journal 2023,* Eastern Shore Writers Association, Inc., c. 2023, p. 15.
6. Noel, *Christmas Faith & Fun,* Fruitbearer Publishing LLC, c. 2014, p. 13.

www.ingramcontent.com/pod-product-compliance
Lightning Source LLC
Jackson TN
JSHW011902240225
79433JS00001B/1

* 9 7 8 1 9 5 6 3 7 0 7 8 2 *